Author:

Jacqueline Morley studied English at Oxford University. She has taught English and history and has a special interest in the history of everyday life. She has written numerous historical fiction and non-fiction books for children.

Artist:

John James was born in London in 1959. He studied at Eastbourne College of Art and has specialised in historical reconstruction since leaving art school in 1982. He lives in Sussex.

Series creator:

David Salariya was born in Dundee, Scotland. In 1989 he established The Salariya Book Company. He has designed and created many new series for publishers in the UK and overseas. He lives in Brighton with his wife, the illustrator Shirley Willis, and their son Jonathan.

Editor: **Karen Barker Smith**
Editorial Assistant: **Michael Ford**
U.S. Editors: **Joanna Callihan** and **Tracey Dils**

McGraw Hill **Children's Publishing**

This edition published in the
United States of America in 2003 by
Peter Bedrick Books
an imprint of McGraw-Hill Children's Publishing
A Division of The McGraw-Hill Companies
8787 Orion Place
Columbus, OH 43240-4027

www.MHkids.com

Library of Congress data is on file with
McGraw-Hill Children's Publishing.

Created, designed and produced by
The Salariya Book Company Ltd
25 Marlborough Place,
Brighton BN1 1UB

Please visit the Salariya Book Company at:
www.salariya.com
www.book-house.co.uk

Printed and bound in Belgium.
Printed on paper from sustainable forests.

ISBN 1-57768-979-8

CONTENTS

The origins of theater	6
Medieval entertainment	8
Traveling players	10
Playing in London	12
England's first theater	14
Running the company	16
Crisis at the Theatre	18
Bankside	20
Inside the Globe	22
The audience	24
The stage	26
Backstage	28
Costumes and props	30
Plague	32
On tour	34
Royal entertainment	36
Fire!	38
Indoor theaters	40
Timespan	42
Glossary	44
Index	45

MAGNIFICATIONS

A Shakespearean Theater

Written by
Jacqueline Morley

Series created by
David Salariya

Illustrated by
John James

PETER BEDRICK BOOKS
Columbus, Ohio

THE ORIGINS OF THEATER

THE IDEA OF A THEATER–a place where live actors perform –is very old and began in the ancient world. The first theaters were holy places, often in front of temples, where priests performed songs and dances to honor their gods. After a time, seating was added along with a kind of stage where performers recreated the sacred legends of the gods. For both actors and audiences these performances were religious ceremonies. People did not go to the theater to be entertained until Roman times.

In the East, just as in the West, theaters arose out of religion. Eastern theaters have kept much closer ties with religion. This Chinese theater (above) was in position in front of a temple c. 1500 A.D. It was a temporary building, probably erected specially for a festival.

The ancient sacred dance, Bugaku, was performed in front of Japanese temples (left). Based on thousand-year-old Asian court dances, Bugaku is still performed on ceremonial occasions, at shrines, and before the imperial court.

Bugaku mask

In early drama, actors wore traditional masks, such as this Japanese Bugaku mask (above), to show the roles they played.

All over the world people worship through dance. Images of Ancient Egyptians, c. 1550 B.C., show them dressed as animal gods dancing in honor of their god Bes (above). The artform known as drama grew out of dances like this.

The first theaters of the western world grew out of arrangements for celebrating the festival of Dionysus, the Ancient Greek god of fertility and wine. A group of men called the chorus chanted songs and danced in a circle surrounding an altar to the god. In 6th-century B.C. Greece, a new ingredient was introduced–single performers who exchanged comments with the chorus. This was how actors and plays came into being. Spectators watched from a semi-circle of open-air seating in Greek theaters.

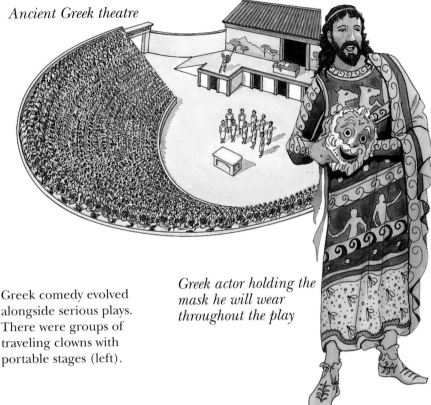

Ancient Greek theatre

Greek actor holding the mask he will wear throughout the play

Greek comedy evolved alongside serious plays. There were groups of traveling clowns with portable stages (left).

Though based on the Greek idea, ancient Roman theaters were much bigger and had no central altar (right). By that time (first century B.C.) theater-going was no longer a religious event. People expected to be entertained. The focus of attention was now the stage, behind which was a wall of elaborate mock buildings from which the actors emerged.

Roman theater c. 55 BC

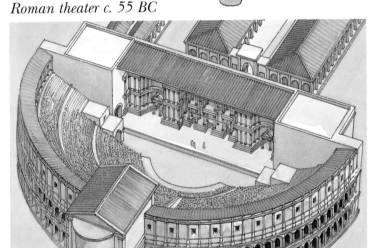

This Ancient Greek "horse" and rider (above), c. 550 B.C., was part of a chorus dancing in honor of the sea god, Poseidon.

Indian temple performers, around the 10th century A.D., worshiped the Hindu god, Krishna (above).

Native Americans of one of the Sioux tribes danced to summon their great Bear Spirit.

Tutsi dancers from Central Africa performed a lion dance to get rid of evil spirits.

MEDIEVAL ENTERTAINMENT

THE EARLY CHRISTIAN CHURCH denounced violence on stage and any form of drama that mocked religion. In the 6th century A.D. the Church closed all theaters. After that, the only entertainers left were the wandering street performers. In time, almost accidentally, the Church itself revived play-acting. In the early Middle Ages, on Church festival days, priests began to enact short scenes from Christian stories during services. Most people at this time could not read so this was a good way of teaching them the stories in the Bible. Each scene was given a simple setting. As the scenes grew in number, settings were put up all round the church. These little plays drew such large audiences they had to be staged outdoors.

At the feast of Corpus Christi scenes telling the whole Bible story took all day to perform. The ways of staging them varied –on fixed stands with audiences going from one to the next, or on wagons that traveled the streets.

In the 15th-century French version of the plays (below), a ring of stands provided both seats for the audience and settings for the action. These included Hell's Mouth and Heaven with a ladder leading up to it. The actors performed in the center.

Actor representing Christ

One of heaven's trumpeters

By late medieval times the actors and musicians performing the scenes were townsfolk rather than priests. There were so many parts to be cast, that local people had to be called in. Soon local people were also organizing the acting and staging.

8

Label

Person dressed as the devil

When local people began taking part they added comedy to the plays. The devil was a favorite comic character.

Scenes were staged on wheeled stands called pageants that were pulled through the town in procession (above). People waited at points along the way for each pageant to stop, give its performance, and move on. In the scene above, the devil has leapt out of Hell's Mouth to defy God's messenger.

With the whole community joining in, the plays grew more elaborate. It became the custom for each of the town's trade guilds to be responsible for staging a scene, usually connected with its members' trade. The goldsmiths performed the Magi bringing gifts (right), the bakers the Last Supper, the shipwrights Noah's Ark, and so on. Some later pageants had machinery for lowering characters from the sky. This was not a new invention. The Ancient Greeks had used similar equipment.

9

A company of wandering players traveled with its cartload of gear (below). They needed only a few costumes and props, food for the journey, and bedding for the night.

Players often set up their stage on a village green (above).

TRAVELING PLAYERS

WHENEVER there was an event that drew big crowds, such as a market in the town square or a Church festival, wandering performers appeared, hoping that people would pay to be entertained. While theaters were banned, generations of actors, acrobats and comedians traveled in search of audiences, wandering from place to place in the carts they used as stages.

By the 16th century, traveling actors were beginning to form themselves into companies to act plays–stories containing several characters. Plays became popular and companies of actors performed wherever they could, upon makeshift stages of boards and trestles.

Wandering beggars (above) were common in 16th-century England.

Many people thought actors were no better than beggars, asking for money for doing nothing of value. Like beggars they were "masterless men". In the Middle Ages, everyone in a useful trade served a master. If you had no master you were seen as being of no use in the world.
Unless they behaved very carefully, players risked being treated like beggars, put in the stocks or driven out of town.

Players in the stocks

10

Occasionally, traveling players managed to talk the lord of a manor into letting them play in the hall of his manor house. If he had heard bad accounts of them, he would send his steward to turn them away. They then had to trudge on to the next town.

Audience member trying to get in without paying

There were more opportunities in a large town. It was quite common to find a bull-baiting or bear-baiting ring, where animals and dogs fought in a bloody duel. These rings were open-air wooden enclosures with viewing stands all around and an entrance door. This made it easier to make sure people paid as they came in. When plays were performed, the audience stood in the central space where the animals normally fought (below).

Curtained changing booth

An inn's yard (below) was another good place to perform. Inns were busy places so there was always a large audience.

Players soon had their stage set up in a yard. Actors entered and exited via a booth at the back, which also served as a changing room (left). Inn audiences were often rowdy and this sometimes earned players a bad reputation. At the next destination, they might be turned away by guards at the town gate (below).

11

PURITANS
AND PLAYERS

PLAYING IN LONDON

The medieval cathedral of St Paul's, the largest in England, had lost its great spire in a fire of 1561.

SIXTEENTH-CENTURY LONDON was a vibrant, growing city. By the 1570s its population of over 100,000 made it one of the largest cities in Europe. It was also one of the richest. Its shops, markets, streets, and inns thronged with traders that made it a magnet for anyone hoping to make a fortune. Among those drawn to London were the companies of players. Some Londoners, especially the conservatively-minded people known as Puritans, were not at all pleased to see so many players. They claimed that play-acting in inn yards caused bad behavior. Plays, said the Puritans, were "the nest of the Devil and the sink of all sins". In spite of this criticism, more and more people flocked to the plays.

St. Paul's Cathedral

Puritans objected to the crowds of rowdy drinkers that plays attracted to the inns.

Puritans claimed people would rather follow a trumpet call to a play than a bell to church.

People living near the inns complained of the constant din from music and fireworks.

With no roof to deaden noise, sound effects like drums and cannon fire were a nuisance.

Playgoers were not the quietest of people. They hissed, stamped, and yelled comments at the players.

The Lord Mayor wrote to the Privy Council about people being injured by falling scaffolds and stages.

The city authorities received constant complaints about the players, especially from the Puritans.

In response the authorities created all sorts of rules designed to keep players out of the city.

12

Cheapside, the largest market, was crammed with country folk selling produce.

Much of 16th-century London was overcrowded and filthy. Its narrow side streets stank with refuse tipped from windows.

The 11th-century Tower of London was a famous landmark. Built by the Normans to keep Londoners under control, it was a fortress, a prison, and a palace.

Tower of London

The London of the 1570s was still ringed by medieval walls. The only way into the city from the south was over London Bridge (below).

London Bridge

13

BUILDING THE THEATER

ENGLAND'S FIRST THEATER

PLAYERS WERE ANXIOUS to show they were respectable. The best way to do this was to persuade a nobleman to be their patron. This meant the players performed for him whenever he wished. In return, they could claim to be one of his "men". They got no pay from him but his title gave them status. One of the best companies of the 1570s was the Earl of Leicester's Men and its manager, James Burbage, was a shrewd businessman. He believed his company could attract much bigger audiences than an inn yard could hold so he proposed a bold idea. He rented some land outside the city walls, where the city council had less control. There he put up a building specially designed for staging plays. This was England's first purpose-built theater.

Burbage shared his brainstorm with his brother-in-law and partner, John Brayne.

The design they created owed a lot to Brayne's experience of fitting up large yards for plays.

Burbage and Brayne borrowed some money and signed a lease to rent the land for 21 years.

The land Burbage rented was in Shoreditch, by a road than ran north from the city. The countryside was still very close to London in those days. Open fields and orchards lay just beyond the city walls. In the surrounding fields, women spread out clothes just washed in the stream (far right). Among the orchards were tenter fields where newly-dyed cloth was stretched to dry (right).

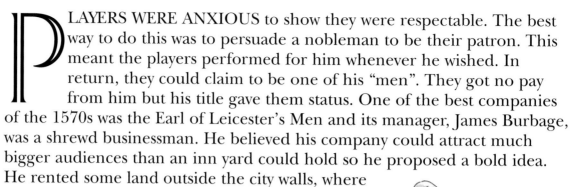

The Theatre's plan may have been based on the practical layout of bear-baiting rings. Like them it had several galleries surrounding a central yard. A platform stage projected into the yard.

The long and expensive oak timbers needed for the framework were cut and fitted at the builder's yard.

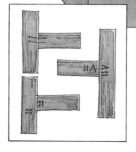

Each piece was marked to show its position. Then the frames were taken apart to be reassembled at the site.

Carpenters on site re-erected the frame by matching the marks. The timbers were joined with wooden dowels.

14

Shoreditch was already a well-known pleasure spot. London families came there on holiday afternoons to see the Tower gunners firing cannon in the Artillery Garden or to watch archery practise in nearby Finsbury Fields (right). Burbage called his new playhouse "The Theatre." It opened in 1576 and was an immediate success.

Completing the theatre walls

Windmill

Until that time, the liveliest feature of Shoreditch had been the whirling sails of nearby windmills.

The frame of the theater was filled with wattle and plastered over. The building appeared circular but was actually formed of many short sides.

The central yard was open to the sky but the galleries were roofed, most probably with thatch.

The interior was described as gorgeous and was probably made of carved and brightly-painted wood.

The stage was probably much like the movable ones of boards and trestles used by traveling players.

There were three tiers of seating around the yard but none in the center. The audience there had to stand throughout each play.

RUNNING THE COMPANY

COMPANY MANAGEMENT

A contract between theater owner and company was often settled over a meal at an inn.

After a performance the takings were counted out and divided into shares.

It is reported that Burbage and his partner had a terrible argument over the takings.

LONDON soon had several more theaters, built by speculators who saw them as a good source of income. In return for letting a company of players use his building, an owner expected to receive half their takings. The other half was divided among the company's "sharers," the people who had provided money to start the company and were entitled to a share in its profits. Sometimes the leading players in a company were also its sharers. They made the decisions about whom to hire, what plays to do, and how to manage the company's budget. The money was spent on costumes, writer's fees, a licensing fee for each new play and wages for the "hired men." These included actors, musicians and people working backstage.

Player and young apprentice

Preparation began early in the new theaters (right). On stage one of the leading players might be coaching his young apprentice, showing him how to stand and move like a woman. Boys played all the female roles because acting was considered a most unsuitable occupation for women.

Writer

Audiences expected a different play every day of the week and wanted new ones all the time. Writers were hired to create plays constantly. Good plays helped to make a company's fortune. Their texts were kept under lock and key so that rival companies could not steal them. Burbage's company was lucky. Its permanent writer was William Shakespeare.

Members of the company read through a new play to decide whether it was worth buying from the author.

The bookkeeper, in charge of the "book" or text of each play was rather like a modern stage manager.

Tiremen looked after the attire (costumes). This took the largest part of the company's budget.

Stagekeepers did all manner of jobs, such as carrying props on stage, wheeling in scenery and keeping things clean.

Musicians with drums and a horn called a sackbut were needed in the plays and for the jig that ended each performance.

16

Theater owners were usually wealthy, while the players tended to be much poorer. Players often borrowed money from the owners. Owners were usually willing to lend it, as they knew they could help themselves to the player's share of the takings as repayment.

Theater owner discussing a loan with a player

AN ACTOR'S CAREER

An actor usually started out at about the age of ten by being apprenticed to a leading player.

The player hired his apprentice to the company. When not acting he was sent on errands.

The previous audience's litter was swept away by one of the stagekeepers (odd-job men). Like the supporting actors, tiremen, musicians and gatherers (who collected the entry money), stagekeepers were hired and had no share in the company's profits.

Young apprentices began with child roles, but would soon have been portraying women most convincingly.

Stagekeeper

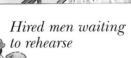

Hired men waiting to rehearse

Hired men (left) played the minor roles in plays. If the company could not afford to employ enough of them, they each had to take several parts in one play.

By his late teens, a young actor had to persuade the company to keep him on for male parts.

17

CRISIS AT THE THEATRE

JAMES BURBAGE had built his Theatre on rented land that its owner had agreed he could use for 21 years. In 1597, the lease ended. When the Burbage family tried to make a new agreement, the landlord refused to sign. He claimed that the Burbages had been bad tenants; they had not stuck to the terms of the agreement and had no further right to the land or the building that stood on it. James Burbage himself was dead by this time and his two sons had inherited the theater. They did not mean to let the landlord rob them of their building. They rented another plot of ground on Bankside, across the river, and hired a builder to pull The Theatre down and cart its timbers over. There they built a new theatre they named the Globe.

Loading timbers for reuse

While the Burbages' workmen were still dismantling The Theatre, the landlord tried to have it stopped. A fight broke out between the Burbages' workers and the landlord's men (right).

Fight between Burbage's and the landlord's men

DISPUTE WITH THE LANDLORD

While the Burbages had been his tenants, the landlord had put up with quite a lot of trouble.

Once, when the landlord's agent came to collect the rent, Burbage's son Richard chased him off with a broom.

Old Burbage had invested in an indoor theater, but neighbours complained and he had been forbidden to use it.

Having nowhere else to act, the Burbage sons had to rebuild. They raised money by selling shares in the new theater.

The most valuable part of The Theatre's structure was its wooden framework. The main timbers were loaded onto carts and taken across the river for re-erection on the new site. These extra-long timbers were expensive and reusing them saved the company a lot of money.

The landlord's agent brought an order from him forbidding demolition of The Theatre. He later sued the Burbages for trespassing on his land, claiming that their men, "armed with many unlawful and offensive weapons", had acted in a "very outrageous, violent and riotous sort."

Landlord's agent

Five leading players in the company agreed to buy shares, meaning the rebuilt theater belonged to all seven.

Meanwhile the Shoreditch landlord sued for damages, complaining about the way the timbers had been hurled around.

He said that trampling feet and carts had ruined his grass. There is no record of how the case was settled.

The landlord did not get ownership of The Theatre as he had hoped. It was rebuilt elsewhere.

King Lear, Act IV Scene V

BANKSIDE

LOCATING THEIR THEATER ON BANKSIDE was a natural choice for the Burbages and their company, the Chamberlain's Men. This area, along the south bank of the Thames, was traditionally where Londoners came to enjoy themselves. It was the place to eat, to drink, to gamble, and to feel free to be as rowdy as they wished. As a result it had a mixed reputation. It was a great place for amusement but also for disorder and crime. Such entertainment was not possible within the city itself where the authorities' rules controlled people's behavior. In 1599, when the Globe Theater opened there for the first time, Bankside already had two competing theatres, the Rose and the Swan. Play-loving Londoners poured across the river to all three, but the Globe soon earned a reputation for excellent plays written by Shakespeare.

There were rows of kennels (below) where dogs were kept for fighting the bulls and bears in the baiting ring.

In the Bear Garden, Bankside's bear-baiting ring, a blind bear was led out to be beaten by men with sticks.

Baiting ring

Rose Theatre

LONDON PLEASURES

Bowling, a favorite 16th-century sport, was not like today's quiet game. Bowling alleys were often also gambling dens.

Bankside had a bull-baiting and a bear-baiting ring where tethered beasts fought until they were exhausted.

Watching dogs fight bulls or bears was considered to be great entertainment.

Cockfighting was another cruel sport that people in those days thoroughly enjoyed and bet upon.

The large number of gambling houses on Bankside was a reason that many people disapproved of the area.

Convicted men from Bankside were taken to the Clink prison not far from London Bridge. They might have been guilty of nothing worse than being a wandering beggar. Still, if they were caught twice, they could be whipped or hanged.

Guard taking a prisoner to the Clink

Medieval London Bridge, covered with shops and houses, was the main road to Bankside. Its southern entrance was protected by a gatehouse topped with battlements. Along these battlements were stakes bearing the rotting heads of executed traitors. The heads served to warn Londoners of the punishment in store for anyone disloyal to the crown.

Globe Theatre

London Bridge linked Bankside (above, as viewed from the southwest) to the city of London on the opposite bank. The Chamberlain's Men's new theater stood next to its rival, the Rose, in open ground next to the lively streets that fringed the river.

Londoners out for a good time were sure to find it. There were lots of places to meet and to dance.

Alcohol in Bankside taverns often led to drunken brawling in the streets.

Bankside attracted cheats and ruffians of all sorts. If caught, culprits were usually flogged.

Though not officially an entertainment, the public execution of criminals always drew large crowds. Seeing someone being hanged was meant to discourage crime.

21

A PLAYER'S DAY

INSIDE THE GLOBE

Players had to be at the theater early in the morning for rehearsal. If they were late, they were fined.

If it started to rain, that afternoon's performance might have to be canceled.

Once the weather cleared the flag was hoisted to proclaim there would be a performance that day.

THE GLOBE was a twenty-sided building. It held around 3,000 people–a big audience for a theater, even by today's standards. No one knows exactly what its interior was like, but judging from a sketch a visitor made of a similar theater, the Swan, it must have looked very much like this (opposite). The players entered through two doors on either side of the stage at the back. These led from the tiring room, a cramped area where players got dressed and waited to come on stage. Between the doors, a small recess, normally hidden by a curtain, served as a stage within the stage. The curtain could be drawn back during a scene to reveal a surprise: people seated at a table, a tomb with a body, or a lurking spy.

People paid a penny (half the price of a pint of good ale) to enter the Globe. Those who wanted to sit paid another penny at the two stairways leading to the galleries. A seat with a cushion cost a further penny.

The illustration (opposite and below) shows the inside of the Globe during a performance of Shakespeare's *Julius Caesar*. Caesar is just about to be murdered. Apart from the large statue pushed on stage especially for the scene, there is no scenery and no curtain to divide the stage from the audience. In the yard people crowded around the stage just as they did in the inn yard performances.

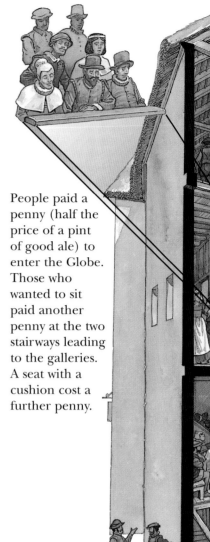

Stage

At rehearsal, players might revise the stage moves of an old play to be performed again that afternoon.

There was no time to stop for lunch so apprentices were often sent out to get everyone pies and ale.

Two o' clock – time for the play to start. From the tiring room a player could peek at the size of the audience.

If a play was late starting, the audience showed their disapproval by hurling nuts and apples at the stage.

A trumpet blast announced that the players were about to begin and everyone became quiet.

Cutaway of the Globe

Gallery

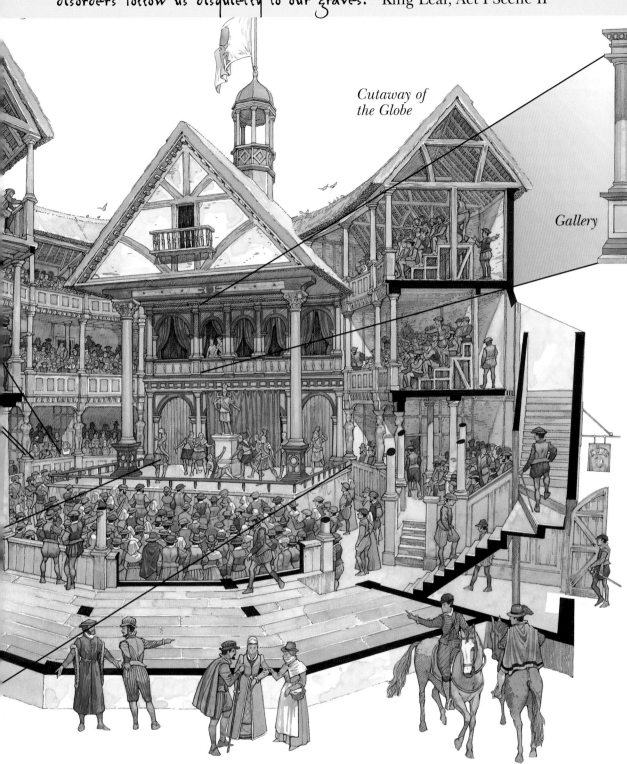

The gallery above the stage (above) was where the musicians usually played. If the gallery was not needed for this, or for battlement or balcony scenes, nobles could sit there to watch the play. They got a good view and avoided mixing with the crowd.

The stage was sheltered by an overhanging roof. The pillars, the rear of the stage, and the ceiling over the stage, were lavishly ornamented. The room in the roof held stage machinery (see page 27).

Backstage, the bookkeeper ensured that each player was ready for his cue and that the props were all to hand.

The tiring men had everything ready to help with quick costume changes between scenes.

Occasionally the writer revised lines at the last minute. With up to 20 new plays a year to learn, players could easily get their lines muddled.

Work was not over when the play ended. The cast often gave a private evening performance in the city.

The end of the day was the first chance to study a new part but players were probably too exhausted by then!

THE AUDIENCE

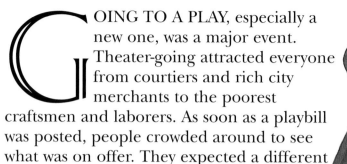

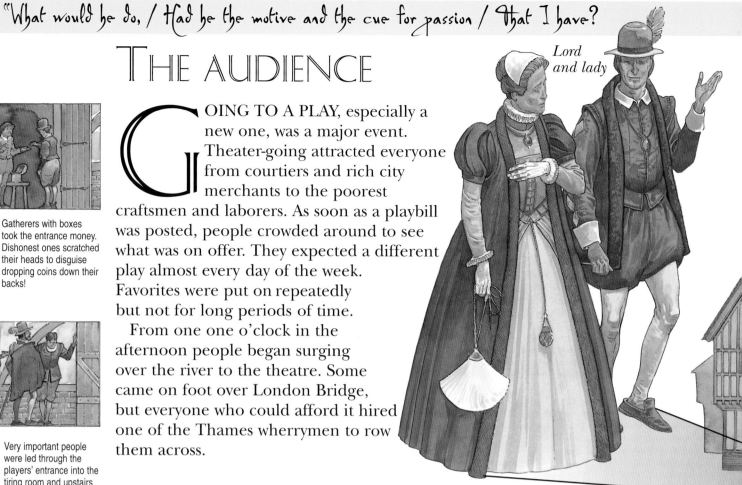

Lord and lady

GOING TO A PLAY, especially a new one, was a major event. Theater-going attracted everyone from courtiers and rich city merchants to the poorest craftsmen and laborers. As soon as a playbill was posted, people crowded around to see what was on offer. They expected a different play almost every day of the week. Favorites were put on repeatedly but not for long periods of time.

From one one o'clock in the afternoon people began surging over the river to the theatre. Some came on foot over London Bridge, but everyone who could afford it hired one of the Thames wherrymen to row them across.

Gatherers with boxes took the entrance money. Dishonest ones scratched their heads to disguise dropping coins down their backs!

Very important people were led through the players' entrance into the tiring room and upstairs to the gallery.

It was a good idea to keep an eye on one's purse. Sixteenth-century clothes had no pockets, so cutting purse straps was an easy job for a thief.

People paid attention if they liked a play but were quick to heckle if they did not.

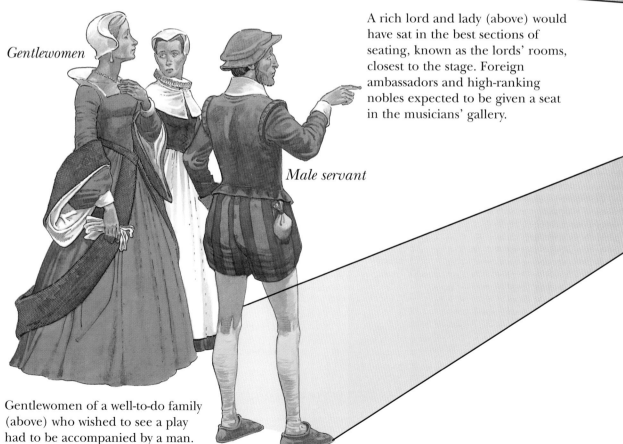

Gentlewomen

Male servant

A rich lord and lady (above) would have sat in the best sections of seating, known as the lords' rooms, closest to the stage. Foreign ambassadors and high-ranking nobles expected to be given a seat in the musicians' gallery.

Gentlewomen of a well-to-do family (above) who wished to see a play had to be accompanied by a man. This was a sign that they were respectable and not to be spoken to by anyone who did not know them. A male servant was enough for this purpose.

Performances were given without an intermission. Bread, ale, and fruit were sold to the audience throughout the play.

Fruit seller

People who stood in the theater yard were called groundlings. Respectable shopkeepers with their families rubbed shoulders with household servants, fishwives, soldiers, seamen, poor artisans, and workmen of all kinds.

Artisans

There were no tickets for performances so people who wanted a good view came early. There was often a lot of jostling to get in. This gave pickpockets the ideal opportunity to get to work. There were lots of them in the crowd.

25

THE STAGE

THE STAGE OF THE GLOBE was basically the platform that traveling players had used but with a permanent roof overhead. As soon as the last of three trumpet blasts warned that the play was starting, the opening players strode onto stage. They had to capture the audience's attention at once, without the help of a rising curtain or dimmed lights. Everything depended on the way they moved and spoke. Voices and gestures had to be commanding, so the style of acting was more exaggerated than we are used to today. Star players drew the crowds. At the Globe, the Chamberlain's Men could count on big audiences for their lead player, Richard Burbage. He was a great tragic actor and was the first to play Shakespeare's great characters, Othello, Hamlet, and King Lear.

Devils or ghosts could spring from the ground through a trapdoor in the stage.

Flinging back the central curtain could reveal a surprise that gave the plot a twist.

The wide side doors allowed big props such as chariots, thrones, and trees to be wheeled on.

For a big procession, even stagekeepers and gatherers had to dress up and come on stage.

The audience loved processions. People in the galleries stood up to get a better view.

Operating the winding gear

Musicians in the gallery

Props

In the gallery, a drummer and a lute player awaited their cues (above). Music, played on lutes, sackbuts, trumpets, and pipes was an important element in most plays and for the jig (comic dance) that was performed afterwards.

There was no stage scenery of the sort we are used to today. The setting of a scene was indicated by bringing an appropriate object on stage, such as a throne, a general's tent, or a box hedge to hide behind.

The same props (left) were used in many plays and were a big part of the company's assets. Carrying or pushing them on and off stage was the job of the stagekeepers.

26

Boy apprentice players were fitted with women's costumes (right) from the tiring men's storeroom. They had to practice walking in a skirt.

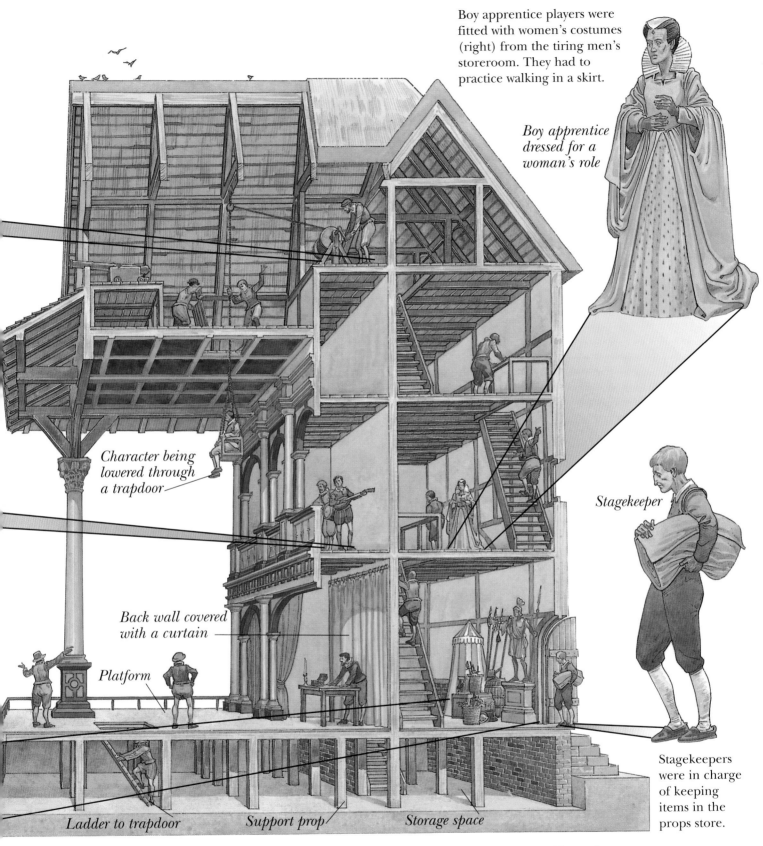

Boy apprentice dressed for a woman's role

Character being lowered through a trapdoor

Stagekeeper

Back wall covered with a curtain

Platform

Ladder to trapdoor   *Support prop*   *Storage space*

Stagekeepers were in charge of keeping items in the props store.

The platform of the stage (above) was at the groundlings' eye level so that they all had a clear view of the players. It was supported with strongly-braced wooden props, allowing for storage space in between. There had to be space left for players to surprise the audience by gaining entry to the stage via a ladder and trapdoor. The underneath of the stage was hidden at the front by boards or by cloth hangings that could be altered to suit the play. The back wall of the stage could be altered too, with tapestries, banners, and painted cloths.

27

conscience of the king." Hamlet, Act II Scene II

SPECIAL
EFFECTS

BACKSTAGE

A hidden bladder of pig's blood was squeezed under the armpit to create the illusion of bleeding.

THE DOORS AT THE BACK OF THE STAGE led into a cramped room where the players got ready and waited to come on. It was known as the "tiring house" because it was related to the players' costumes or "attire." In the tiring house, clothes hung and tiremen made last-minute adjustments to the players' costumes. Tables and benches were covered with parts to learn, written out on long rolls of paper, drums and armor, false beards, wigs, and make-up. The bookkeeper was in charge in the tiring house and ensured that the stagekeepers assembled the right props for each play and that the players needed for each scene were dressed and knew their cues. Throughout the performance he was ready, with the play in his hand, to prompt players if they forgot lines.

Thunder was sounded by a roll of drums or a cannonball rolled over a sheet of metal.

Stagekeeper

Birdsong was created by blowing through a pipe into a jar of water.

Stagekeepers checked that the yard was full and the rest of the audience was seated before giving the go-ahead to the trumpeter on the stairs. The trumpeter then ran up to the roof to sound the opening trumpet blast.

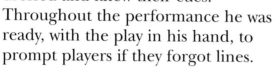

A beheading needed a special split-top table. Its sides were covered with a cloth or boards.

In the space above the stage (known as the heavens) a player acting the part of a god could wait for his cue.

A drumroll of thunder disguised the creaks of the winding gear as the player descended from the clouds.

Below the stage, in the region known as "hell," a player in the role of a ghost could wait to rise from a tomb.

He had to duck sideways as the trapdoor fell, to avoid getting a nasty bump on the head.

Trumpeter

A flight of steps led from the tiring house to the storerooms on the upper floors. This was where the company's stock of costumes, properties, and texts of plays were kept. They were very valuable and were kept under lock and key. The upper floors also housed the winding gear and the turret from where the theater's flag was hoisted.

THE BOOKKEEPER'S JOB

The bookkeeper had to get each play licensed by an official called the Master of the Revels.

Players studied the plot of the day's play to help them keep track of what they had to do. The plot was a summary that the bookkeeper made and kept handy. It noted who was in each scene and when they were due on and off stage. As each day's play was different from the last, players needed this reminder!

Stairs to upper floors

He then employed a scrivener (a professional copyist) to write out all the parts.

If not on stage in a particular act, Shakespeare could continue working on a text (below). His major contribution to Burbage's company was the two plays a year he wrote for it. Few playwrights employed by companies had such a good reputation.

Hired men often had to be several characters in one play. The bookkeeper organized this.

Shakespeare at work

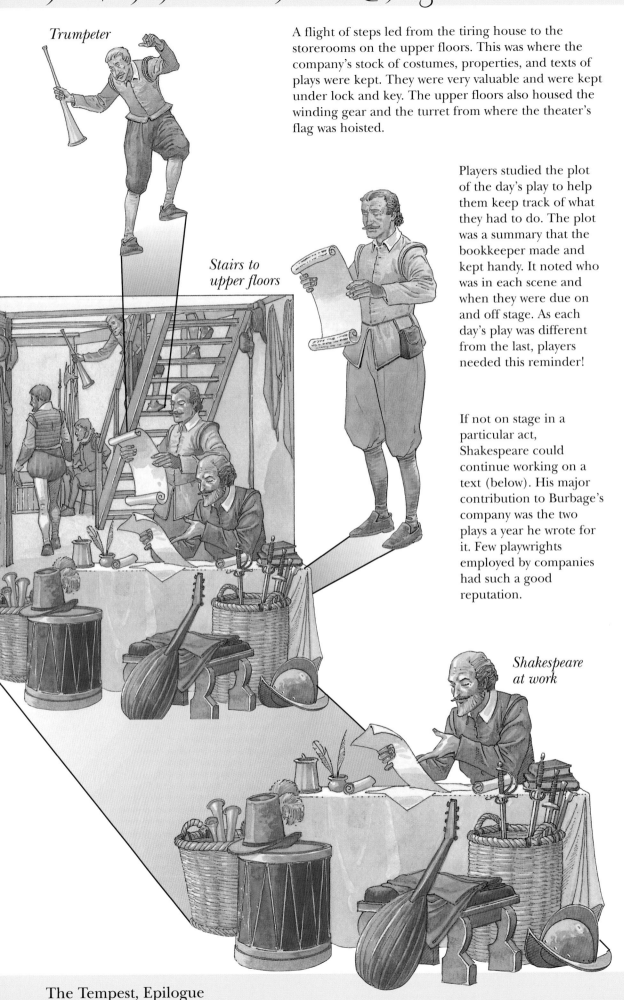

He recorded all production details to ensure performances ran smoothly.

The Tempest, Epilogue

COSTUMES AND PROPS

Gold-embroidered jacket

COSTUME was a company's biggest expense. The clothing had to be luxurious–people in those days were used to seeing magnificently-dressed processions in the streets, such as the Lord Mayor and his officials, great nobles and their servants, or Queen Elizabeth I and her attendants. The stage kings, queens, and nobles had to look just as fine in the glare of the public, in broad daylight. Very often the players really were wearing the clothes of the court. Fashions changed so fast that, after wearing them only a few times, nobles gave exquisite silk garments to their servants to sell to the theaters. No wonder that players could be punished severely for leaving the theater still dressed in their costumes!

In the tiremen's workshop (right) last minute work was done on costumes for the new play being performed the next day. One or two of the players may have needed a final fitting. Old costumes might be remodeled to fit new players. Costumes brought out of storage needed checking to ensure moths had not ruined them. Completed garments were hung ready on a rail.

Headgear (right) was an important part of any costume. At this time everyone always wore some form of head covering, even in bed.

Helmet for a pikeman

Felt hat

Gentleman's pearl-encrusted leather glove

Costumes were so essential that companies would borrow money to buy them and promise to repay the loan with future takings.

We know from theater accounts that tiremen spent large sums on fabric and trimmings.

They would certainly have been on the look out for servants offering their employers' clothes for sale.

Its costumes were a company's most valuable possession. They were kept carefully in locked chests.

These two players (right) are shown having been fitted out with some magnificent second-hand clothes from court. The man wears a jewel-encrusted long-skirted doublet over a suit of star-spangled armor. His fur hat is topped with ostrich feathers, the ultimate luxury.

The rigid shape of 16th-century women's fashions made it easy to give a boy a woman's figure (far right). Their bodies were imprisoned in conical-shaped corsets with whalebone reinforcements and their skirts were held out over stiffened frames, called farthingales.

Ostrich feathers

Player dressed as a nobleman

Boy dressed as a noblewoman

Jewel-encrusted doublet

There is a record of a company paying twenty pounds, ten shillings and sixpence for a black velvet cloak "with sleeves embroidered all with silver and gold, lined with black satin striped with gold." This was at a time when the average wage of a schoolteacher was fifteen pounds a year.

A tawny coat that was damaged by rats had to be mended with eight pounds in weight of copper lace.

Found on a company's property list: Neptune's fork and garland, Cupid's bow, hell's mouth, and the cloth of the sun and moon.

People's ideas about the clothes of past ages were vague but there was an attempt at historical dress, such as a Roman general (above left) and medieval costumes for a masque, or danced entertainment (above right).

In bad plague years there were so many deaths that bodies were collected nightly from households. They were piled onto carts and taken away to burial pits because there was no time to give each a separate grave.

Face covered for fear of catching the disease

Houses where there had been plague deaths were marked with a red cross warning people not to enter (below). The occupants were not allowed to come out for fear they would infect others. Food was passed to them through the windows.

Ships from abroad carrying infected rats first brought the plague to London.

The plague was believed to be God's way of punishing the sinful. This print (above) shows death dancing on the coffins of Londoners and makes a prayer for mercy.

We now know that the plague was spread to humans by fleas.

PLAGUE

LONDONERS FEARED the deadly illness known as the plague, which returned to the city regularly. Between 1592 and 1625 there were five particularly terrible plague years, in each of which 10% of the city's population died. At that time nobody understood what caused the plague but they knew it spread rapidly when lots of people were crowded together. Theaters and bear-baiting rings drew big crowds, so the authorities closed them down until the number of plague deaths had fallen below 50 a week (30 in some years) for three weeks running. When the summer heat brought a return of the disease, theater companies were forced to load up their carts, leave London, and return to the life of traveling players.

The fleas picked it up from the huge population of rats in London.

People thought pomanders (spice-scented balls), held to the nose, gave protection from plague.

In the worst plague years few people were given the luxury of a coffin (above). Many bodies were flung into pits as they were.

Foul air was thought to spread diseases so fires were lit to purify it.

Lime was put in the burial pits to help the piles of bodies rot.

Notices announcing the closure of theatres were posted up on playhouse walls.

The coughing of those infected spread the plague, so banning large crowds was a good idea.

Everyone who could fled London. Players' wagons joined the queues leaving the city.

The fewer men, the greater share of honour." Henry V, Act IV Scene III

ON TOUR

HAVING TO GO ON TOUR was not a positive move for the players. To meet the costs of travel, companies cut down on the numbers going, so many hired men lost their jobs. Those that joined the tour had to manage on rough food and lower pay, or no pay at all if audiences were poor. Some companies went abroad, while others tried their luck in towns and villages at home, traveling long distances and lodging in uncomfortable drafty barns and lofts. Players usually entered each town with a great display of merriment, but often they received an unfriendly welcome. People feared they might have brought the plague with them and they were not allowed to perform unless the town mayor gave his permission. If he refused he might give them some money anyway, out of respect for their noble patron. The mayor was really paying them go away.

A helpful mayor might have paid for a show and invited leading citizens as his guests.

If the mayor was worried about the plague he was more likely to have turned the players away.

A manager whose company acted when forbidden to was thrown into prison.

Turned out of town without a bed, players had to spend the night under their cart.

To make sure that everyone in town heard about them, players made a really noisy arrival. The whole company paraded through the streets, singing catchy tunes and dancing merrily.

A small touring company of nine men enter another town

To make a good first impression, the head of the company waved a banner showing the coat of arms of its noble patron. This might have persuaded the local constable to let the players in through the town gates.

A trumpeter and a drummer led the way, making as much noise as they could, while the company's clown performed all sorts of tricks and cracked jokes with onlookers. If he could make them laugh, they were more likely to come to see him in the show.

Head of the company

Company's clown juggling for the crowd

Trumpeter

35

ROYAL ENTERTAINMENT

UNLIKE THE DISAPPROVING officials of the City of London, Queen Elizabeth I enjoyed watching plays. It was not customary in those days for kings and queens to go to performances at public theaters. Instead, the Master of the Revels, the official in charge of royal entertainment, arranged for the players to come to court. At festive times, such as Christmas, New Year, and Shrovetide, the queen expected lavish entertainments to keep herself and her courtiers amused. These might include half a dozen or more plays. Ensuring a ready supply of well-rehearsed plays for the court was the official reason for allowing companies of players to exist in the first place. Their public performances in theatres were officially classed as "rehearsals" for their "real" work–entertaining royalty or their noble patrons.

Only the best companies were called to court. The Chamberlain's Men from the Globe were the queen's favorites and were asked to play twice as often as any other company. At Christmas 1596, for instance, they performed all six command performances.

Queen sitting beneath the royal canopy

Household official

As part of the Christmas festivities at Greenwich Palace, the queen asked the Chamberlain's Men to perform for her (opposite). They hoped for her approval of *Romeo and Juliet*, a new play by William Shakespeare.

The audience was assembled according to each person's rank. The queen, sitting beneath a canopy symbolizing royal power (above), took center place. Less important people, such as the household official, were not given seats. It was not appropriate for them to sit in the queen's presence.

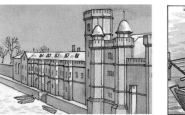

Queen Elizabeth called the players to whichever palace she was using at the time, perhaps Whitehall or Greenwich.

The players and their gear arrived by boat. Rowing along the Thames was the quickest way to get about at that time.

The Master of the Revels was told about the plays proposed to make sure the queen would like them.

For several days workmen were busy making a temporary stage and putting up festive decorations.

Important audience members

Other important audience members, such as a visiting foreign ambassador and his wife (left) and leading nobles, were seated at the front beside the queen.

Romeo and Juliet is pictured, below, drawing to its tragic end. Friar Lawrence came to Juliet's tomb to rescue the lovers, but arrived too late. The role of the Friar (right) might well have been played by Shakespeare himself. He was an actor in the company, though there is no record of which parts he played.

Player in the role of Friar

The great hall of the palace had a screened-off passage at one end with two entrances and, above it, a minstrel's gallery. By putting up a platform it easily became a theatre. Much the same arrangements were made in medieval times when wandering players performed in the halls of manor houses.

Romeo and Juliet provided the sort of corpse-strewn action that Elizabethan audiences loved. Romeo kills his rival, Paris, and takes his own life believing Juliet to be dead. Waking from a death-like sleep, Juliet kills herself in grief.

The queen expected to be pleased and amused. She did not allow religious or political matters to be mentioned in plays.

After the performance the players were treated to a lavish meal and plenty to drink before going home.

James I, who was crowned in 1603, was a great lover of plays. He spent much more on them than Elizabeth had.

James made his favorites, the Chamberlain's Men, his personal players. They were renamed the King's Men.

FIRE!

THE PLAYERS AT THE GLOBE, through royal favor renamed as the King's Men, continued to attract large audiences to Bankside. One of their successes in 1613 was a play about Henry VIII in which Richard Burbage, the company's leading player, played the king. The performance on June 29th provided more spectacle than anyone had bargained for. When King Henry arrived at Cardinal Wolsey's house, the cannon fire that greeted him set the theater on fire. A spark landed on the thatched roof and set it smoldering. The fire traveled quickly, though no one noticed it. A whiff of burning was nothing unusual in the theater. Guns and fireworks were routinely set off to liven up the action.

Once fire took hold in a wooden building there was little hope of stopping it. There were no organized fire departments in those days. Within a couple of hours, the whole building had burned to the ground. The King's Men at once set about rebuilding their theater on its old foundations. By the following summer a second Globe had opened. By all accounts, it was even more splendid than the first.

The Globe had only two exits, at the foot of the two stair turrets. The audience–probably over 2,000 people–was lucky to have had enough time to escape.

People who had arrived by boat found themselves taking to the river again sooner than they had expected (right). The Thames would have been a handy source of water to put out the blaze if there had been any way of pumping it to the fire.

When a new play at the Globe was advertised with Burbage in the lead, there was a lot of interest.

Crowds flocked to the theater. By now the King's Men were the most popular players in London.

The cannon was probably fired from just below the thatch. There were no fire regulations in those days.

The smoky smell may have been disguised by the smell of tobacco. Smokers in the audience puffed on pipes throughout performances.

We have quite a good idea of what the new Globe (right) looked like. A view of Bankside drawn in about 1640 shows the outside of the theatre and the twin gables over the stage. We can only theorize about what the interior looked like.

One man's pants reportedly caught fire but the blaze was put out by drenching them with ale!

When they realized the danger, people in the galleries jostled to get down the stairs to safety.

The only method of getting water to the fire was to pass buckets from hand to hand in a human chain.

Builders were soon at work recreating the theater, with certain improvements. This time the roof was made of tile.

INDOOR THEATERS

JAMES BURGAGE SENIOR had originally created an indoor theater from a hall in what had been Blackfriars priory, a small monastery (see page 18). The great halls of wealthy people's houses had traditionally been the place for private performances and this probably gave him the idea. Open-air theaters were not much use in winter. Burbage also determined that if there were fewer seats, people would pay more for them. Local residents objected to a public theater at first. By 1608 attitudes had changed and the highly respected King's Men were allowed to reclaim their theater. They spent summers at the Globe and winters at Blackfriars, which became London's first fully-professional indoor theatre.

Blackfriars Theater (below) as it probably looked around 1608. It held about 800 people, all of whom were seated. Seats were quite expensive. The cheapest cost sixpence, about half an average London worker's weekly wage. The audience was smaller and made up mostly of the upper classes.

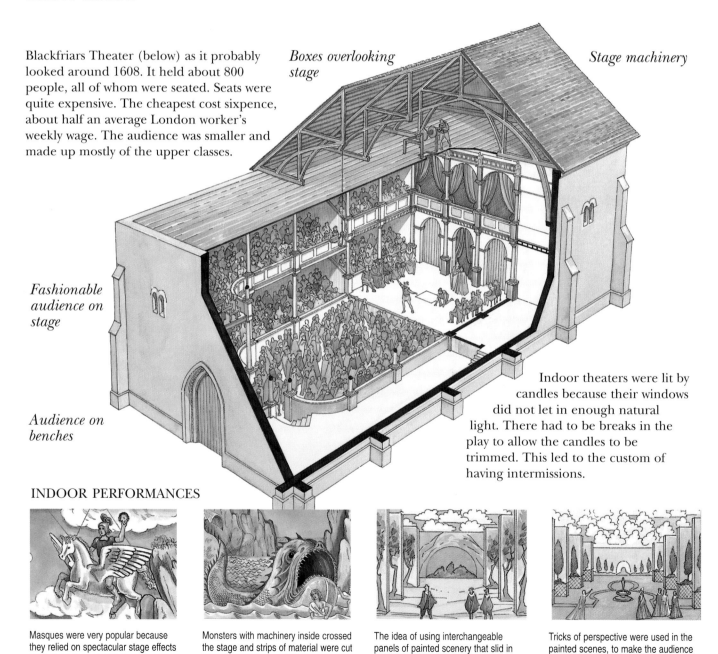

Boxes overlooking stage

Stage machinery

Fashionable audience on stage

Audience on benches

Indoor theaters were lit by candles because their windows did not let in enough natural light. There had to be breaks in the play to allow the candles to be trimmed. This led to the custom of having intermissions.

INDOOR PERFORMANCES

Masques were very popular because they relied on spectacular stage effects such as gods appearing from the sky.

Monsters with machinery inside crossed the stage and strips of material were cut into waves and moved like the sea.

The idea of using interchangeable panels of painted scenery that slid in and out originated in Italy.

Tricks of perspective were used in the painted scenes, to make the audience feel they were looking into an open space.

Private indoor performances reflected the taste of the court and the nobility at the time, who enjoyed elaborate danced entertainments known as masques. Masques were performed for James I at Whitehall (above). The popularity of masques influenced the sort of entertainment that 17th-century public theatres provided and the spectacular scene changes required in masques affected the way theatres were designed.

Drury Lane Theater was built in 1674. The stage (right) had much greater depth to allow for many panels of sliding scenery at the sides. There was a changeable backcloth instead of a rear wall with doors. Actors entered from between the panels instead of through doors in the back.

To increase the illusion of looking into a picture, the inner stage was framed by an arch called a proscenium.

Strict Puritans, who denounced theater-going, became more influential in the 17th century.

When the Puritans gained power in the English Civil War they had theaters destroyed. The Globe was demolished in 1644.

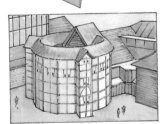

Today on Bankside a replica Globe Theater, opened in 1997, stages Shakespeare's plays in the setting he knew.

41

TIMESPAN

c. 2300 B.C. An ancient document of this date in the British Museum refers to a religious ceremony in which priests enacted the deeds of the gods.

c. 1000 B.C. The ancient Greeks honored Dionysus, god of wine and fertility, in a festival of wild dancing. During the following centuries dance-drama became part of these festivals.

6th century B.C. By this time, the festivities for Dionysus had become formal ceremonies of dance and song performed by a chorus of 50 men. Prizes were given for the best song.

534 B.C. According to tradition, Thespis, a priest of Dionysus, won the competition in this year by introducing a performer who exchanged comments with the leader of the chorus. This produced the first dialogue in the history of the theater.

c. 500 B.C. Outdoor theaters with tiers of stone seating and a performance area developed. Earlier arrangements had wooden seating for the audiences at these ceremonies.

From 27 B.C. Roman theaters in the Roman Empire, modeled on those of Greece, staged increasingly extravagant and violent entertainments.

312 A.D. The Roman Emperor Constantine was converted to Christianity. Laws were passed banning cruel entertainment.

410 A.D. Theaters throughout the Roman Empire were closed after the sacking of Rome by Alaric the Visigoth.

975 A.D. Drama was introduced into the service for Easter Sunday at the monastery of St. Gall, Switzerland.

Player in the role of Jesus

1264 A.D. Pope Urban IV established the church festival of Corpus Christi in June. It soon became the greatest day of the year throughout Europe for the performances of religious plays.

1501 A.D. At Mons, in what is now Belgium, the Corpus Christi plays needed 67 different settings in the market place. They took 48 days to rehearse and four to perform.

15th-16th centuries A.D. Meanwhile, professional troupes of traveling entertainers were developing "interludes" (short plays) as part of their routines.

Gallery above the stage

1564 A.D. Birth of William Shakespeare in Stratford-upon-Avon, England.

1572 A.D. Parliamentary Act for the Punishment of Vagabonds (wandering beggars) required every company of players to be authorized by a noble patron.

1570s City authorities began to complain that acting in inn yards caused disorder.

1576 A.D. James Burbage of the Earl of Leicester's Men

built The Theatre, the first professional public playhouse in the modern world.

c. 1588 A.D. Shakespeare came to London and joined the company at The Theatre.

1592 A.D. London suffered the first of many terrible plague years during this period.

1594 A.D. Shakespeare was named as one of the players in Burbage's company (now the Chamberlain's Men) who acted before Queen Elizabeth I at Christmas.

Important audience members

1596 A.D. James Burbage converted part of old Blackfriars Priory in London into an indoor theater but was not allowed to use it.

1596 A.D. The reputation of the Chamberlain's Men was so high that the queen asked them to give all six of her Christmas command performances.

1597 A.D. James Burbage

died. The Theatre (and the unusable Blackfriars) then belonged to his sons, Richard and Cuthbert. The lease of The Theatre expired.

1598 A.D. Landlord disputes led to The Theatre being pulled down and re-erected on Bankside as the Globe, financed by leading members of the Chamberlain's Men.

1599 A.D. Opening of the first Globe Theater, where most of Shakespeare's greatest plays were performed. A German visitor, Thomas Platter, attended a play and his impressions, recorded in his journal, provide evidence of what Elizabethan theaters were like.

1603 A.D. Death of Elizabeth and accession of James I. Making himself patron of the Chamberlain's Men, he renamed them the King's Men.

1608 A.D. The King's Men were allowed to use their building in Blackfriars as an indoor public theater. From then on they performed in summer at the Globe and in winter at Blackfriars.

1613 A.D. The Globe Theater was destroyed by fire but rebuilt and reopened by the following year.

1616 A.D. Death of William Shakespeare.

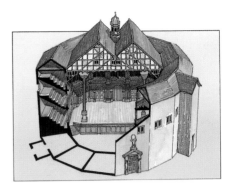

The new Globe, built in 1614

1619 A.D. Death of Richard Burbage.

1619 A.D. The Teatro Farnese in Parma, Italy, was the first theater to be built with a proscenium opening framing its stage.

c. 1620 A.D. Painted panels of scenery (called flats), sliding in grooves, were introduced in Italy, to create swift scene changes.

1642-1660 A.D. Civil War in England. The Puritans ordered all theaters to be closed.

1644 A.D. The second Globe was demolished.

1970 A.D. American Sam Wanamaker launched a campaign to build a replica of the first Globe Theater as close as possible to its original site on Bankside.

1997 A.D. First full season of performances at the new Globe.

43

GLOSSARY

Apprentice An unpaid trainee craftsman, serving a master craftsman for a fixed number of years, in return for free training.

Artisan A craftsman or mechanic.

Bear-baiting The sport of dogs fighting a chained bear in an arena. Bull-baiting, a similar entertainment, was also popular in Elizabethan times.

Canopy A covering suspended over a throne or held over a person in a procession.

Chorus A group of singers and dancers in a religious festival. In ancient Greek drama the chorus expressed the feelings suggested by the action of the play.

Cockfighting Setting two roosters to fight each other to the death and betting on which would survive.

Constable An official of a parish or town appointed to keep peace and order.

Corpus Christi A Christian festival established by Pope Urban IV in the 13th century. It is celebrated on the first Thursday after Trinity Sunday.

Cue Words or action in a play that serve as a signal for another actor to speak, or a property or sound effect to be produced.

Dowel A headless wooden pin that joins two pieces of wood by penetrating both.

English Civil War The war that began in England in 1642 between the supporters of Charles I and those who opposed his policies. It led to the execution of King Charles in 1649 and the establishment of a republican state which lasted until the restoration of the monarchy in 1660.

Fishwives Women who served at fish stalls in markets.

Gatherer A person who collected the audience's money at the theater door.

Guild An association of people of the same craft or trade, formed to help and protect its members.

License Permission, issued by the government in return for a fee. Both Elizabeth I and James I were worried that plays might contain speeches that might make people rebellious. Granting or refusing a license for a play was a way of censoring it or of raising tax.

Magi The three wise men who brought gifts to the infant Jesus.

Patron An important person who agrees to use his influence to protect others in return for certain services.

Plague Bubonic fever, so called because it caused "buboes" (swellings) in the groin and armpits.

Playbill An advertisement for a play.

Pomander A mixture of sweet-smelling spices, made into a ball and carried by a person as a protection against infection.

Portable Able to be carried.

Priory The dwelling of a community of friars, who were members of religious orders. Their buildings were confiscated by Henry VIII which explains why premises in Blackfriars were available for conversion.

Proscenium arch The large opening in the wall that separates the seating area from the acting area in a conventional theater, through which the audience sees the stage. It was introduced in Italy in 1619 and became a regular feature of European theaters.

Puritans People who believed in living a very simple life, based on Biblical teaching. They rejected the authority of bishops, who were supported by the King. This was one of the causes of the English Civil War.

Sackbut A bass trumpet, with a slide like that of a trombone for altering the pitch.

Shrovetide The Sunday, Monday and Tuesday before Ash Wednesday. In the 16th century there were a number of festivities just before Lent. Lent, which begins on Ash Wednesday, is the Christian period of fasting before Easter.

Stagekeeper A stagehand who was expected to do all sorts of other jobs, from caretaking to playing walk-on roles.

Tawny Cloth of a brownish color.

Tenter field Open-air space in which lengths of newly-dyed cloth were hung to dry, tautly stretched on lines.

Tiremen Hired men in charge of costumes.

Wattle Thin strips of wood interwoven with twigs or flexible canes to form a panel.

Whalebone A horny substance found in the jaw of certain whales. Strips of it were used to stiffen clothes.

Wherrymen The men who rowed wherries, rowing boats that acted like taxis, across the River Thames.

INDEX Page numbers in bold refer to illustrations

A
apprentices 16, 17, 24, 25, 27
audiences 16, 22, 24, 25, 26, 37, 38, 40

B
Bankside 18, 20, 21, 38, 39, 41
bear-baiting rings 11, 14, 20, 33
beggars 10, **10**, 21, 42
Blackfriars Theater 40, **40**, 43
bookkeeper 16, 23, 28, 29
Brayne, John 14
Burbage, James 14, 18, 42
  Richard 18, 26, 36, 43

C
Chamberlain's Men 20, 21, 26, 36, 37, 43
changing booth 11, **11**, 22, 28
Cheapside 13
chorus 7
Christian Church 8
Civil War 41, 43, 44
cockfighting 20, 44
Corpus Christi festival 8, 42
costume 16, 28, 30-31, **30-31**

D
Dionysus 7, 42
Drury Lane Theater 41, **41**

E
Earl of Leicester's Men 14
Elizabeth I 30 36, **36**, 43

F
farthingales 31
fire services 38

G
Globe Theater 18, 20, **21**, 22, 23, **23**, 26, 27, 38-39, **38-39**, 43
  modern Globe 41, 43
  second Globe 38-39, 40, 41, 43
Greenwich Palace 36
groundlings 25
guilds 9 44

H
hired men 15

I
inn yards 11, **11**, 42

J
James I 37, 43

K
King's Men 37, 38, 40

L
licensing 16, 44
London 12-13, **12-13**, 14, 16
London Bridge 20-21, **21**, 24
Lord's rooms 24

M
masques 40, 41
Master of the Revels 36
musicians 23, 26
musicians' gallery 23, 24

P
pageants 9, **9**
patrons 14
plague 32, **32**, 33
plots 29
pomanders 34
Poseidon 7
proscenium arch 41, 43
props 26, **26**, 31
public executions 21
Puritans 12, 41

R
Romeo and Juliet 36, 37
Rose Theater 20-21

S
St. Paul's Cathedral 12
scenery 26, 39, 41
Shakespeare, William 16, 20, 29, 36, 42, 43
sharers 16
Shoreditch 14-15
special effects 28, **28**
speculators 16
stage 14, **17**, 26-27, **27**
  portable 7, **7**, 8-9, **9**, 10-11
stagekeepers 16, 17, 22, 26, 27, 28
stocks 10, **10**
Swan Theater 20, 22

T
temples 6
tenter fields 14, 44
theaters
  Ancient Egyptian 6
  Ancient Greek 7, 9, 42
  Chinese 6, **6**
  indoor 40-41, **40-41**
  Japanese 6, **6**
  Medieval 8, 9, 42
  owners 15, 17
  Roman 7, **7**, 42
  takings 16
The Theatre 14, **15**, 18-19, **19**
  design and construction 14, 15
tiremen 16, 30
tiring room 22, 24, 28, **28**
Tower of London 13, **13**
traveling players 7, 10, **10-11**, 15, 33, 34-35, **34-35**, 36, 42

W
Wanamaker, Sam 43
Whitehall palace 36
winding gear 9, **9**, **26**, 28-29
windmills 15
writers 16-17